READING POWER

Mia Hamm
Soccer Superstar
Heather Feldman

The Rosen Publishing Group's
PowerKids Press ™
New York

1

For Sophie Megan

Published in 2001 by The Rosen Publishing Group, Inc.
29 East 21st Street, New York, NY 10010

First Edition

Book Design: Michael de Guzman

Photo Credits: p. 5 © Al Bello/ALLSPORT; p. 7 © Jamie Squire/ALLSPORT; pp. 9, 17 © Rob Tringali Jr./SportsChrome USA; p. 11 © Office of Sports Information, University of North Carolina; p 13 © Mike Cooper/ALLSPORT; p. 15 © Andy Lyons/ALLSPORT; p. 19 © Brian Bahr/ALLSPORT; p. 21 © Vincent Laforet/ALLSPORT.

Feldman, Heather.
   Mia Hamm : soccer superstar / Heather Feldman.
      p. cm.— (Reading power)
   Includes bibliographical references and index.
   Summary: This book introduces Mia Hamm, one of the top female soccer players in the world.
   ISBN 0-8239-5716-0
   1. Hamm, Mia, 1972- —Juvenile literature. 2. Soccer players—United States—Biography—Juvenile literature. 3. Women soccer players—United States—Biography—Juvenile literature. [1. Hamm, Mia, 1972- 2. Soccer Players 3. Women—Biography] I. Title. II. Series.
   2000   00-027219
   796.334'092—dc21
   [B]

Contents

Mia Hamm plays soccer.
Mia is a great soccer
player.

5

Mia kicks the soccer ball hard. She kicks the soccer ball into the goal net. Mia scores a goal.

Mia can jump high.
She jumps up to get
the soccer ball.

Mia played soccer in college. Her team was called the Lady Tarheels. Mia helped the Lady Tarheels win all four years she played.

Mia also played on the
United States Olympic
Team in 1996. The
Olympic Games were in
Atlanta, Georgia, that year.
Mia and her team won the
gold medal.

On May 22, 1999,
Mia scored her 108th
international goal.
International means
with other countries.
This was a record.

Lots of people love Mia. She is a great soccer player and a great person. Her fans let her know how much they love her.

Marvelous Mia!

By Morgan Robinson *mia #1 fan!*

Many of Mia's fans ask for her autograph. They want to remember meeting Mia forever.

In 1999, Mia played for the United States in the Women's World Cup. Mia and her teammates won the World Cup. This made them the best women's soccer team in the world.

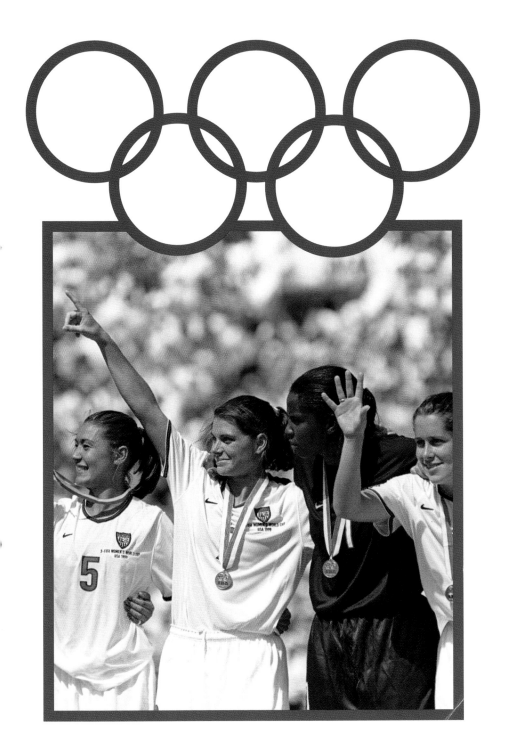

Glossary

autograph (AW-tow-graf) When a person signs his or her name for another person.

goal (GOHL) When you put the ball in the other team's net. In soccer your team gets one point for a goal.

Olympic Games (oh-LIM-pik GAYMZ) A world sports competition.

player (PLAY-er) A person who plays in a game.

record (REK-urd) When a player or team does something better than any other player or team ever has.

scores (SKORZ) When a player gets a point for a team.

soccer (SOHK-er) A sport where two teams kick and pass the ball without using their hands. Each team tries to get the ball into the other team's net.

Women's World Cup (WUH-munz WURLD KUP) A soccer competition, played by women every four years, to decide which team is the best in the world.

Here is another good book to read about Mia Hamm:

Mia Hamm: Good as Gold
by Mark Stewart
Children's Press

To learn more about soccer, check out these Web sites:

www.yahooligans.com/Sports_and_
    Recreation/Soccer
www.womensoccer.com

Index

Word Count: 173

Note to Librarians, Teachers, and Parents

If reading is a challenge, Reading Power is a solution! Reading Power is perfect for readers who want high-interest subject matter at an accessible reading level. These fact-filled, photo-illustrated books are designed for readers who want straightforward vocabulary, engaging topics, and a manageable reading experience. With clear picture/text correspondence, leveled Reading Power books put the reader in charge. Now readers have the power to get the information they want and the skills they need in a user-friendly format.

24